Hip-hop USA

Hip-hop Fashion

Sue Vander Hook

Consultant:
Emmett G. Price III, PhD
Chair, Department of African American Studies
Associate Professor of Music and African American Studies
Northeastern University
Boston, Massachusetts, USA

www.raintreepublishers.co.uk
Visit our website to find out
more information about
Raintree books.

To order:
☎ Phone 0845 6044371
📄 Fax +44 (0) 1865 312263
💻 Email myorders@raintreepublishers.co.uk

Customers from outside the UK please telephone +44 1865 312262

Raintree is an imprint of Capstone Global Library
Limited, a company incorporated in England and
Wales having its registered office at 7 Pilgrim Street,
London, EC4V 6LB – Registered company number:
6695582

Text © Capstone Press 2011
First published in the United Kingdom in hardback
  by Capstone Global Library Ltd in 2011
Paperback edition first published in the United
  Kingdom by Capstone Global Library Ltd in 2012
The moral rights of the proprietor have been asserted.

Edited by Diyan Leake
Designed by Ashlee Suker
Originated by Capstone Global Library Ltd
Printed in and bound in China by Leo Paper
  Products Ltd

ISBN 978 1 406 21824 4 (hardback)
14 13 12 11 10
10 9 8 7 6 5 4 3 2 1

ISBN 978 1 406 22181 7 (paperback)
15 14 13 12 11
10 9 8 7 6 5 4 3 2 1

British Library Cataloguing in Publication Data
Vander Hook, Sue
Hip-hop fashion. – (Hip-hop USA)
A full catalogue record for this book is available from
the British Library.

Acknowledgements
We would like to thank the following for permission
to reproduce photographs: Alamy/PYMCA, 6; Brian
Chase/123RF, 15 (top); Capstone Studio/Karon Dubke,
13, 14 (all), 16 (top and bottom), 20, 41; Corbis/Atsuko
Tanaka, cover; DVIC/Howard R. Hollem, 22 (top);
Getty Images Inc./Al Pereira/Michael Oachs Archives,
19, 26; Getty Images Inc./Florian Moser/Stock4B,
9; Getty Images Inc./Frederick M. Brown, 31; Getty
Images Inc./Gautam Narang, 29; Getty Images Inc./
Michael Ochs Archives, 36, 39, 40; Getty Images Inc./
Scott Gries, 18 (bottom), 33; iStockphoto/andyjibb,
28; iStockphoto/Xsandra, 8; Jeffrey Banke/123RF, 23;
Landov LLC/Ron Wolfson, 25 (bottom); Newscom,
22 (bottom), 27 (bottom), 34; Newscom/AFP
Photo/Timothy A. Clary, 44; Newscom/KMazur/
WireImage, 45; Newscom/PNP/WENN, 27 (top);
Newscom/UPI/Ezio Petersen, 32; Newscom/UPI
Photo/Laura Cavanaugh, 12; Newscom/WENN/
Jody Cortes, 43; Newscom/WENN/Ken McCoy, 35;
Olga Savchenko/123RF, 15 (bottom); Shutterstock/
Alexander Kalina, 7 (pink belt); Shutterstock/alias
(old wall background throughout); Shutterstock/
averole (splash element throughout); Shutterstock/
ayakovlevdotcom, 5 (dancer), 21 (top); Shutterstock/
Cyriel, 21 (bottom left); Shutterstock/dendong,
7 (coat); Shutterstock/Dooley Productions, 37;
Shutterstock/Elke Dennis, 10; Shutterstock/Idigital,
18 (top); Shutterstock/James Steidl, 42; Shutterstock/
JJJ, 11; Shutterstock/John A. Anderson, 5 (graffiti);
Shutterstock/kolosigor, 16–17; Shutterstock/lev radin,
4; Shutterstock/Lucian Coman, 25 (top); Shutterstock/
MAT, 24; Shutterstock/Meliksetyan Marianna, 7 (legs);
Shutterstock/pandawan, 38 ; Shutterstock/Petrov
Stanislav Eduardovich (cement wall background
throughout); Shutterstock/Pokaz (black banner
element throughout); Shutterstock/Sergey Peterman,
7 (orange belt); Shutterstock/WilleeCole, 21 (bottom
right).

Every effort has been made to contact copyright
holders of material reproduced in this book. Any
omissions will be rectified in subsequent printings if
notice is given to the publisher.

Disclaimer
All the Internet addresses (URLs) given in this book
were valid at the time of going to press. However, due
to the dynamic nature of the Internet, some addresses
may have changed, or sites may have changed or
ceased to exist since publication. While the author
and publisher regret any inconvenience this may cause
readers, no responsibility for any such changes can be
accepted by either the author or the publisher.

CONTENTS

How it began

Shoes with fat laces. Oversized hoodies. Jeans that hang low. Hip-hop fashion wasn't created in a designer's studio. In the 1970s, it began on the streets of the Bronx, a New York City **borough**. This was a time when hardship and unemployment gave birth to art, music, and dance.

FASHION IN THE BIG APPLE

New York is known as the "Big Apple". The city has been a fashion hot spot for many years. Fashion Week, New York's most important fashion event, kicked off in 1993. Each year, designers from around the world flock to Fashion Week to show off their lines.

In 2006, the Museum of the City of New York honoured hip-hop fashion. The **exhibit**, called Black Style Now, featured clothing worn by P. Diddy, Lil' Kim, and LL Cool J.

Young people who lived in this mostly African-American and Latino borough expressed themselves in many ways. **Graffiti** artists painted on buildings and train carriages. MCs wrote rhyming lyrics to pump up the crowds at street parties. **Breakdancers** spun on their heads to the beat of the street-corner **DJ**. No matter how they expressed themselves, hip-hoppers used fashion to stand out from the crowd.

borough ▶▶ one of the five divisions of New York City

graffiti ▶▶ letters or pictures painted, scratched, or marked onto a piece of public property

5

Hip-hoppers in the 1970s dressed in whatever they had. Some breakers danced in jogging bottoms and T-shirts, while others danced in nylon tracksuits. MCs wore tight jeans and bomber jackets.

By the 1980s, rappers like Kurtis Blow and Big Daddy Kane had become hip-hop royalty. They added custom-designed suits, heavy gold chain necklaces, and multi-finger rings to their look. The more **bling** they wore, the more successful they appeared.

bling flashy jewellery sometimes worn to show wealth

CHIC MEETS HIP-HOP

In September 1991, a Chanel fashion runway show in New York City was a mix of chic and hip-hop. Models strutted down the catwalk in flowing chiffon dresses. But they also wore big gold chains, wide flashy belts, fishnet stockings, and black leather jackets. The event was a benefit to raise money for disadvantaged New York teens.

As hip-hop became more popular, people wanted to be part of it. Millions wanted the music, but they also wanted the look. The styles that began on the streets developed into a multibillion dollar fashion industry.

CHAPTER 1

Clothing & Footwear

Hip-hop styles began with young people of the inner city. They wanted to stand out, so they wore what no one else was wearing. A one-of-a-kind outfit drew praise and boosted the wearer's confidence.

JEANS HANGIN' LOW

Jeans have always been a staple of the hip-hop look. In the 1970s and 1980s, slim-fitting jeans were popular with both men and women. Some DJ and graffiti crews painted their names down the legs of their jeans.

Levi Strauss & Co. invented denim blue jeans in 1873.

In the 1990s, baggy jeans replaced slim jeans in many hip-hoppers' wardrobes. The jeans hung down around the hips with no belt. Prison-issue trousers were often too big and fell down around the hips. Because belts could be used as a weapon, prisoners weren't allowed to have them to hold up their trousers. Some hip-hoppers copied the prison look to appear tough. They bought the best dark denim jeans they could afford, in two or three sizes too big.

In the 2000s, hip-hop jeans that were fitted around the waist with wide legs gained popularity with men. Rocawear, a fashion line started by rapper Jay-Z, and P. Diddy's Sean John brand offered this jean style. Women's jeans became fitted with slim legs.

T-SHIRtS & HOODiES

T-shirts were standard hip-hop fashion from the start. Some were airbrushed with graffiti-inspired art. In the late 1980s, rap group Public Enemy talked about social and political topics in their songs. Soon, T-shirts were printed with strong social messages and **rebellious** statements. And then there were hip-hoppers who preferred tank-style vests. They often paired these shirts with matching T-shirts.

The early 1990s saw hip-hop T-shirts go bright and bold. Los Angeles clothing company Cross Colours came out with baggy T-shirts in bright colours. Hip-hop group Kris Kross made the clothing famous in the video for their 1992 song "Jump". Female rap and R&B group TLC also sported Cross Colours T-shirts.

Hip-hop T-shirts crossed over into the **preppy** look in the late 1990s. Polo shirts in bright colours such as blue, yellow, and even pink became popular. Today, rappers such as T.I. and Kanye West wear the preppy look in their music videos and on the red carpet.

In 1994, Snoop Dogg appeared on *Saturday Night Live* wearing a Tommy Hilfiger sweatshirt. The next day, the sweatshirt sold out of stores throughout New York.

Hip-hoppers began sporting huge hooded sweatshirts and sports jerseys in the 1990s. Eminem put on an oversized hoodie and low-riding tracksuit bottoms to create the look he is still known for. In the 2000s, designers punched up the hoodie look with bright colours and all-over prints.

rebellious ❯❯ *disobedience to the people in charge*

preppy ❯❯ *a style of dress made up of classic clothing and a neat appearance*

WHATEVER Suits You

Breakdancers, also called b-boys and b-girls, danced in nylon tracksuits back in the 1970s and 1980s. The slippery material helped them twirl and slide.

By the mid-1980s, MCs and DJs caught the tracksuit bug. Rap group Run-DMC favoured the Adidas tracksuit. Velour tracksuits became popular near the end of the decade.

Jay-Z

As rap music became more successful in the 1990s and 2000s, the hip-hop look changed. Rappers like the Notorious B.I.G. and Jay-Z wanted a more high-class image. They often dressed in expensive suits.

TiME FOR JaCKEtS

In the 1970s and 1980s, hip-hoppers walked the streets in jackets made of sheepskin, leather, denim, and fur. Many rappers, DJs, and graffiti artists painted their crew names on the backs of their jackets. Today, down jackets, leather coats, cropped jackets, and even fur coats are still popular in hip-hop fashion.

A GOOD SPORt

The Starter brand jackets were first made for professional sports teams like the Raiders and the Bulls. But they later became popular hip-hop attire.

1971 — The Starter company is founded in New Haven in the state of Connecticut.

1980s — Starter brand clothing line partners with major-league sports teams to make team jackets and caps.

1991 — The film *Boyz N the Hood* comes out, starring rapper Ice Cube. The movie features Starter clothing, which helps make the brand more popular with hip-hop fans.

Late 1990s — The popularity of Starter jackets fades.

2009 — Starter pays the Dallas Cowboys quarterback Tony Romo to help make the brand more popular.

13

THESE BOOTS ARE MADE FOR WALKING

Heavy suede Timberland brand work boots became part of hip-hop fashion in the 1990s. Rapper and record producer Timothy Mosley adopted "Timbaland" as his stage name. The Wu-Tang Clan, Boot Camp Clik, Jay-Z, and others rapped about Timberland boots in their songs.

As hip-hop fashion became more distinctly male and female, women's boots went in a variety of directions. Some women stuck with the Timberland work boot look. Others took the glamorous, high-fashion route. They wore ankle-high, knee-high, and over-the-knee boots.

StiLEttoS

One of the favourite shoe and boot styles of female hip-hoppers is stilettos. Stilettos have high, thin heels. Heel height can range from 7.6 centimetres (3 inches) to more than 15 centimetres (6 inches). They make legs look long and strong.

Late 1500s — Heeled shoes first appear in Western Europe.

Late 1600s — King Louis XIV of France wears red heels. Only French royalty are allowed to wear red heels.

1950s — Stilettos become all the rage. The styles of French designer Robert Vivier are very popular. The *Daily Telegraph* newspaper reports on a stiletto heel that is 9 centimetres (3½ inches) high. These high-heeled shoes have metal shafts in the heels.

Mid-1960s — As flats become more common, the stiletto's popularity fades.

1970s — Designer Manolo Blahnik reintroduces the stiletto design.

1990s — The popularity of stilettos is revived by rappers such as Lil' Kim and Foxy Brown.

2000s — Stilettos are a fashion must-have.

15

CRAZY ABOUT TRAINERS

Even more important than boots in hop-hop fashion are trainers. B-boys and b-girls started wearing trainers in the 1970s and 1980s. Clean white shoes proved that a breaker had skills. Only "bad" dancers scuffed their trainers.

Soon the trainer trend caught on with other New York City teens. Popular trainer brands in the 1980s included Nike, Converse All Stars, Pro-Keds, Adidas, and Pumas. Because some kids couldn't afford more than one pair, cleanliness became key. Kids used toothbrushes to keep their trainers looking new. Others painted their old shoes to make them look new again.

Time to change up the look of a trainer? No problem. Hip-hoppers used wide laces to match the colour of their hats and T-shirts. Ironing these "phat" laces helped make them even wider.

Some hip-hoppers left the laces out of their shoes. They were copying the prison look. Prisoners weren't allowed to have shoelaces.

The trainer craze spread beyond New York City to the rest of the United States in the mid-1980s. Nike released its popular red and black Air Jordan trainer in 1985. Basketball superstar Michael Jordan wore them in every game. Air Jordans first became popular with rappers, who passed the style onto their fans.

Today, custom-designed trainers are popular in hip-hop fashion. Some artists paint one-of-a-kind shoes for their customers. They paint anything from family members to film posters on the shoes.

In the early 1980s, the National Basketball Association (NBA) didn't allow red or black trainers. They fined Michael Jordan each time he played in a pair of Air Jordans.

Hip-Hop Hits MTV

In the 1970s and 1980s, kids living in big cities such as New York and Los Angeles grew up around hip-hop culture. They listened to the music and copied the hip-hop fashions they saw every day. But kids living in small towns and rural areas didn't hear or see much hip-hop.

All that changed when *Yo! MTV Raps* debuted on MTV in 1988. *Yo!* helped spread hip-hop music and fashion to small towns across America. The programme was hosted by Andre "Doctor Dre" Brown, James "Ed Lover" Roberts, and Fred "Fab 5 Freddy" Braithwaite. It was MTV's first hip-hop music show. America's youth liked the music. They also wanted to copy the hip-hop styles they saw on TV. Hip-hop fashion was no longer just an inner-city trend. It was for anyone.

Ed Lover

Fab 5 Freddy

Doctor Dre

YO! MTV FASHION

>> Members of the rap group Run-DMC hosted the pilot episode of *Yo! MTV Raps*. They wore black fedora hats, gold chains, black shirts, and dark jeans.

>> Female rap group Salt-N-Pepa appeared on the show's first episode. They wore gold jewellery and acid wash jeans.

A BIT OF AFRICA

In the late 1980s, rappers such as Queen Latifah, A Tribe Called Quest, and De La Soul added African traditions to their styles. They used fashion to show they were proud of their African **heritage**. These African styles included shirts and hats made of kente cloth. The clothing was often red, black, and green. Many African flags have these colours in them.

Queen Latifah

CHAPTER 2

Hats, hair, & bling

Hip-hoppers are always very bold with their accessories. They often top off their look with a hat, a fresh new hair style, or a shiny piece of bling.

>> Kangol hat

Hip-Hop Hats

In the 1980s, Kangol hats were all the rage with hip-hoppers. Rappers like Run-DMC and LL Cool J wore Kangol hats. Slick Rick even formed a rap group called the Kangol Crew. One member of the rap group U.T.F.O. had so many Kangol hats that he was called the Kangol Kid.

Baseball caps have been popular with sports fans for decades. But rappers made them into hip-hop style in the 1990s. They wore them tilted, turned to the side, and backward.

In the 1990s and 2000s, some rappers added fedora hats to their looks. Rappers such as Jay-Z, the Notorious B.I.G., and LL Cool J sported these broad-brimmed felt hats.

SPORTiNG A DO-RAG

For hundreds of years, people have wrapped cloth, called do-rags, around their heads. At first, do-rags served a purpose. Some farmers and other workers used do-rags to soak up sweat during hard labour. In World War II (1939–1945), women working in factories used do-rags to keep their hair out of the machinery. African-Americans stretched do-rags over their heads to create waves in their hair or to keep their cornrows in place.

Tupac's bandanna
In the early 1990s, Tupac Shakur sported a bandanna wrapped around his head and tied in front.

IT'S AN ISSUE

From its music to its fashion, hip-hop has had its critics. Some in the hip-hop community worry that hip-hop has become too focused on money and material things. DJ Kool Herc, known as the father of hip-hop, spoke out against rap stars who promote an expensive lifestyle. "It ain't about keeping it real," he said. "It's got to be about keeping it right". Herc encouraged rappers to use their music and fame to help spread positive messages of hope and responsibility.

Today, hip-hoppers have turned do-rags into a fashion statement. Some people wear them alone. Others add a baseball cap, knit hat, or fedora hat on top.

23

FASHION HAIR

Hairstyles have always been important in the hip-hop community. From afros to dreadlocks, hip-hoppers turn heads by rocking these stylish 'dos.

» cornrows — hair braided (plaited) in rows very close to the scalp

trendsetters — ODB and Method Man of Wu-Tang Clan, Snoop Dogg

» hair weaves — long strips of hair; the hair can be glued to the scalp or sewn into or braided into the natural hair.

trendsetters — Lil' Kim, Da Brat

» shaved head

trendsetters — LL Cool J, Rakim

CORNROW ART

Actress Cicely Tyson made cornrows popular on her TV series *East Side/West Side* in 1963. The style remained a favourite among African Americans throughout the 1970s.

By the 1990s, hip-hoppers began making cornrows into an art form. The variety of designs ranges from simple straight braids to spiral patterns. Cornrow styles can take hours to complete. But with the right care, the hairstyle can last a month or more.

>> **dreadlocks** — ropelike strands of hair formed by matting or braiding the hair

trendsetters — Lauryn Hill, Lil Wayne

>> **afro** — tight curls styled in an evenly rounded shape

trendsetters — Ice Cube, Questlove

>> **jheri curls** — glossy, loose curls

trendsetters — Eazy-E, Kurtis Blow

>> **caesar** — short hair with a fringe over the forehead

trendsetters — Eminem, Ludacris

Fresh Prince

>> **hi-top fade** — a tall afro with the sides cut very short; a hi-top fade that leans to one side is called "the gumby".

trendsetters — Fresh Prince, Kid 'n Play, Big Daddy Kane, Tupac Shakur

25

Rockin' the Bling

The bling look began with long, heavy gold chains in the 1980s. Rappers Kurtis Blow, Big Daddy Kane, and Run-DMC helped make these chains a staple of hip-hop fashion.

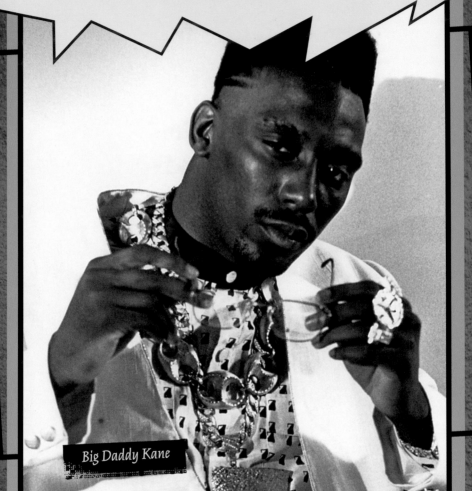

Big Daddy Kane

By the 1990s, hip-hoppers added flashy pendants to their chains. These huge diamond-studded plates often spelled out a person's name. Even belt buckles got a kick of bling. They sometimes displayed names in gold, **platinum**, or even diamonds.

platinum ≫ *a very valuable silver-white metal often used in jewellery*

WORLD'S BIGGEST BLING

Rapper Lil Jon's "Crunk Ain't Dead" pendant is the largest diamond pendant in the world. It was added to the Guinness World Records in 2007.

Weight: 2.3 kilograms (5 pounds)

Height: 19 centimetres (7½ inches)

Width: 15 centimeters (6 inches)

Number of diamonds: 3,756

Cost: $500,000

GRILLZ

Gold and jewels moved to the teeth in the 1980s. They were called grillz. The most expensive grillz were inlaid with precious jewels. Rappers such as Flavor Flav, Big Daddy Kane, and Kool G. Rap were among the first to add grillz to their looks. By the 2000s, Lil' Flip, T-Pain, and Nelly helped turn grillz into a fashion statement as well as a status symbol.

Flavor Flav

27

EARRINGS, BRACELETS, & RINGS

Huge hooped earrings, called doorknockers, became a favourite with female hip-hoppers in the 1980s. Rappers such as Roxanne Shante and Salt-N-Pepa helped make these oversized hoops popular. The earrings were big and heavy, but they weren't always made of real gold or diamonds.

CELEBRITY BLING

Where do the hip-hop stars buy their bling? One of the hottest hip-hop jewellery stores is Jacob & Co. in New York City. The store began as a small stall. In the mid-1990s, singer Faith Evans recommended the store to her husband, the Notorious B.I.G. Soon other rap stars began wearing the jewellery. Today, celebs like P. Diddy, 50 Cent, Madonna, Beyoncé, and Justin Timberlake sport bling from Jacob & Co.

What's that bling?
The term *bling* started in the southern United States. In the late 1990s, Southern rappers Lil Wayne and B.G. sang about bling in their hits "Millionaire Dream" and "Bling Bling". In 2003, the word was included in the *Oxford Dictionary*. In 2006, the word was added to the US *Merriam-Webster* dictionary.

Heading into the 1990s, hip-hop bling moved to the wrists, fingers, and hips. Thick gold bracelets, rings, jewelled belts, and gold chains around the hips became hip-hop hits. Big, colourful sunglasses embedded with jewels were popular with men and women. Some hip-hoppers added diamond piercings to their fashion statements.

CHAPTER 3

Selling the look

As the hip-hop look spread, some fashion designers and rap artists started clothing lines. They based their fashions on everyday hip-hop styles.

KARL KANI

In 1989, Karl Kani became the first fashion designer to make hip-hop clothing available to the general public. His oversized jeans were popular with hip-hoppers. They no longer had to buy their jeans two or three sizes too big.

TIME FOR KARL KANI

1989 — Karl Kani opens his first store on Crenshaw Boulevard in Los Angeles, California.

1991 — Rapper Dr. Dre helps promote the brand.

1999 — The Karl Kani collection is shown at the White House to President Bill Clinton and Vice President Al Gore.

2001 — Karl Kani launches Kani Ladies, a fashion line for women.

2002 — Karl Kani wins the Urban Fashion Pioneer Award at the Urban Fashion Awards in New York.

Karl Kani

The key to Kani's success was getting the right people to wear his clothes. He outfitted Tupac Shakur, the Notorious B.I.G., Snoop Dogg, and the Fresh Prince. People saw what these stars were wearing and wanted the same look. Wearing Karl Kani clothes became a sign of success. In just two months, Kani's business exploded. He went from shipping a few thousand pieces of clothing a month to 3 million items a month. He became known as the "Ralph Lauren of the streets".

URBAN CLOTHING LINES

Other designers were quick to catch on and start their own hip-hop lines. They brought hip-hop style to people from all walks of life.

>> **1992 — Phat Farm** Russell Simmons, co-founder of Def Jam Records, starts Phat Farm clothing for men. The mixture of urban and preppy catches on. He later expands the line by adding Baby Phat, a clothing line for women.

>> **1992 — FUBU**
Daymond John founds FUBU, a clothing line made for and by African Americans. FUBU means "For Us, By Us".

>> **1998 — Sean John**
Founded by rapper Sean "P. Diddy" Combs, Sean John is one of the top-selling hip-hop lines for men. In 2004, P. Diddy wins the Council of Fashion Designers of America's award for Menswear Designer of the Year.

>> **2004 — Respect M.E.**
Missy Elliott partners with Adidas to release her Respect M.E. fashion line for women. The line includes trainers, tracksuits, jackets, and T-shirts.

>> **2003 — Apple Bottoms** Rapper Nelly establishes Apple Bottoms, a popular hip-hop fashion line for women. Celebs such as Fergie, Ashanti, and Oprah wear the brand.

>> **1999 — Rocawear** Jay-Z and his business partner Damon Dash start an urban clothing brand called Rocawear. The line caters to both men and women. Rocawear becomes one of the top-selling hip-hop fashion lines.

TO tHE RESt OF tHE WORLD

Hip-hop designers and clothing companies didn't hesitate to market their styles worldwide. They shipped to other countries and sold their fashions online. Anyone in the world could then dress hip-hop. People in Japan especially took hold of hip-hop fashion. Japanese designers created their own hip-hop fashion lines.

In 2004, Japanese fashion designer Nigo, right, teamed up with rapper and producer Pharrell Williams, left, to launch the hip-hop fashion line Billionaire Boys Club.

Daymond John

THE BIRTH OF FUBU

In 1992, Daymond John searched all over New York City for a tie-top hat. When he found one for $20, he was shocked by the high price and the poor quality. John decided to make and sell his own hats. His mother taught him how to sew. John sat at a sewing machine every day to make his tie-top hats.

The first day John took to the streets to sell his hats, he earned $800. His mother soon moved out of her house. She let John turn it into a clothing factory. Within two years, FUBU offered baggy jeans, aviator jackets, down coats, and an assortment of headwear. Each piece had the embroidered FUBU logo. Today, FUBU is popular around the world.

CHAPTER 4

Style stars

LL Cool J

LL Cool J burst on to the hip-hop scene in 1985 with his hit single "I Can't Live Without My Radio". LL, whose nickname stands for "Ladies Love Cool James," has maintained a successful hip-hop career for more than 20 years. Whether it's a beret, fedora, or do-rag, LL is rarely seen without a hat.

LL Cool J was the first celebrity to help sell the FUBU brand.

LL launched his clothing line, Todd Smith, in 2006. His collection features graphic hoodies and T-shirts for men.

Run-DMC

Run-DMC changed the face of hip-hop music with the 1983 singles "It's Like That" and "Sucker MCs". Many rappers of the early 1980s used funk and disco styles in their songs. Run-DMC scaled back their sound to just drums and a **turntable**. The group's hard-hitting look was just as powerful as its new sound.

In 1986, Run-DMC gave a shout out to their favourite trainer in the song "My Adidas". After the song's release, Adidas Superstars sales skyrocketed. That autumn, Adidas executives attended a Run-DMC concert. When the band played "My Adidas," thousands of fans held up their Adidas shoes. Adidas soon paid Run-DMC $1 million to **endorse** their trainers.

turntable — *circular, revolving surface used for playing phonograph records*

endorse — *sponsor a product by appearing in advertisements*

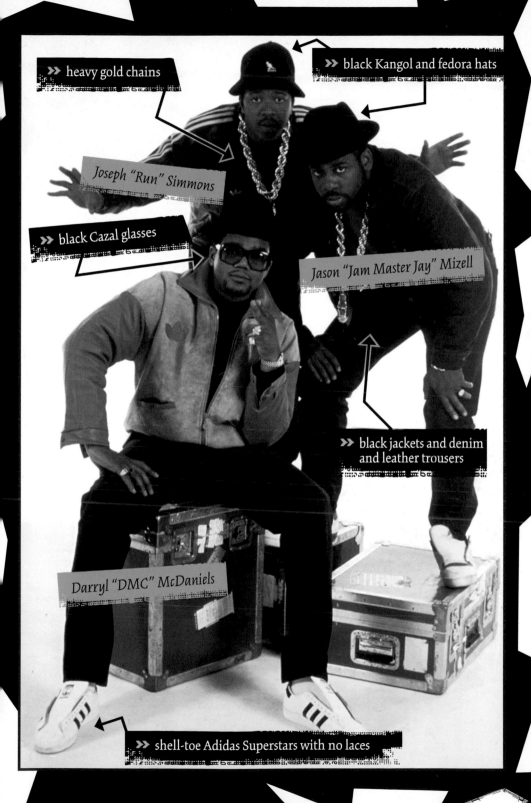

heavy gold chains

black Kangol and fedora hats

Joseph "Run" Simmons

black Cazal glasses

Jason "Jam Master Jay" Mizell

black jackets and denim and leather trousers

Darryl "DMC" McDaniels

shell-toe Adidas Superstars with no laces

Salt-N-PEPA

Salt-N-Pepa entered the rap scene in 1985 with the single "The Show Stopper". After selling more than 8 million albums, Salt-N-Pepa is considered the greatest female rap group of all time. They changed female hip-hop fashion from rough and tough to glitzy and revealing.

>> asymmetrical haircuts

>> big gold chains

>> doorknocker earrings

Cheryl "Salt" James

Sandy "Pepa" Denton

Dee Dee "DJ Spinderella" Roper

>> tight-fitting acid wash jeans

1980s FASHION

The 1990s saw Salt-N-Pepa sporting black floppy hats and polka-dot tops. They wowed fans while wearing hot pants, cut-off denim shorts, and Lycra body suits.

1993 album

Entertainment Weekly magazine listed the 1980s fashion of Salt-N-Pepa as one of the 50 Pop-Culture Moments That Rocked Fashion.

asymmetrical >> *unevenly shaped*

EARLY FEMALE MCs

The first female rappers wore a mix of tough and glitzy fashions. They wanted to look strong in a male-dominated industry. But they also celebrated being female by adding bling and showy fashions to their looks.

» **Sha-Rock** was the first female **MC** to be part of a well-known crew. She started out as part of the rap group the Funky 4 + 1. In 1981, they were the first rap group to appear on *Saturday Night Live*. Sha-Rock wore a mix of plain black clothing, wild stripes, and bright colours.

» **Roxanne Shante** came on the scene in 1985 with her hit single "Roxanne's Revenge". Shante's style included gold doorknocker earrings, leather jackets, and even boxing gloves.

» **MC Lyte** began rapping at the age of 12. In 1986, she released her first single, "I Cram to Understand U". MC Lyte sported a denim jacket, huge gold chains, doorknocker earrings, and rings on every finger.

SLICK RICK

Long before rap artists wore diamond necklaces and grillz, rapper Slick Rick rocked the bling. Slick Rick moved from England to the Bronx in the late 1970s. He soon formed the rap duo Kangol Crew with rapper Dana Dane. In 1988, Slick Rick signed a solo contract with Def Jam Records. He is considered one of the best writers in hip-hop music.

Slick Rick was known for adding a lot of gold and diamond jewellery to his look. Dripping with gold chains, diamond rings, and his signature eye patch, Slick Rick became known as the "godfather of bling". He even wore a crown.

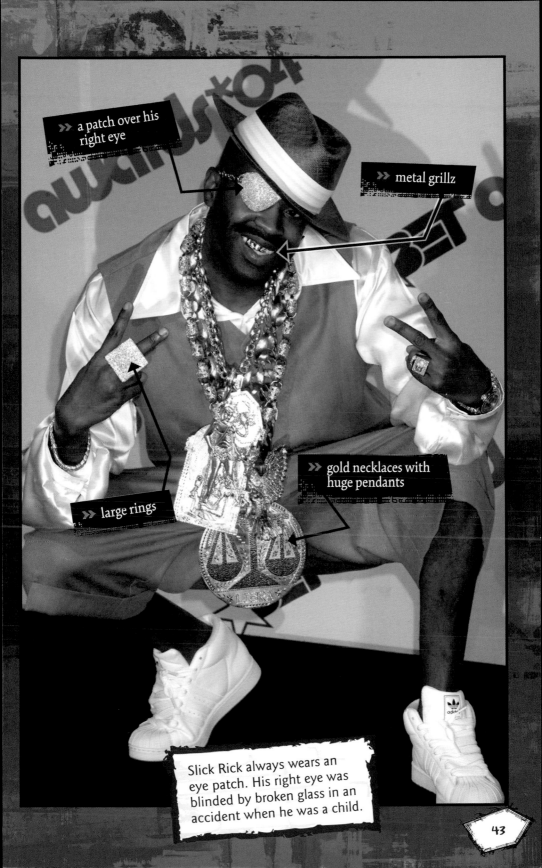

» a patch over his right eye

» metal grillz

» large rings

» gold necklaces with huge pendants

Slick Rick always wears an eye patch. His right eye was blinded by broken glass in an accident when he was a child.

ANDRÉ 3000

From the time he was a teenager, rapper André 3000 didn't want to dress like everyone else. He dyed his jeans wild colours such as blue and orange. In the early 1990s, he formed the hip-hop group OutKast with his high school friend Big Boi. OutKast drew attention for their catchy tunes and André's unique fashion sense.

» wigs

>> golfer hats, straw hats, and fedoras

>> ties and bow ties

>> preppy vests and sweaters

Best Dressed
In 2005, André 3000 made it on to *Vanity Fair* magazine's International Best-Dressed list.

In 2008, André took his love of fashion to the next level. He started his own fashion line called Benjamin Bixby. The fashions include preppy styles inspired by US student clothes of the 1930s. André draws the fashion designs himself.

FASHION FORWARD

From the hippie looks of the 1960s to the rocker fashions of the 1970s, music inspires fashion trends. Hip-hop has changed the face of fashion like no other style of music. What began on New York City streets is now in high demand across the globe. From trainers to jeans to jewellery, hip-hop fashion will continue to shape the way people dress.

GLOSSARY

asymmetrical unevenly shaped

bling flashy jewellery sometimes worn to show wealth

borough one of the five divisions of New York City, each of which is also a county

breakdancer dancer of a form of street dance that features footwork, floor work, and acrobatic moves

DJ person who plays pre-recorded music for a radio, party, or club audience

endorse sponsor a product by appearing in advertisements

exhibit display that shows something to the public

graffiti letters or pictures painted, scratched, or marked onto a piece of public property

heritage history and traditions handed down from the past

MC person who rhymes to the DJ's mix, connecting with the audience in a performance

platinum a very valuable silver-white metal often used in jewellery

preppy a style of dress made up of classic clothing and a neat appearance

rebellious disobedient to the people in charge

turntable circular, revolving surface used for playing phonograph records

FiND OuT MORE

BOOKS

Cornish, Melanie J. *The History of Hip Hop*, Crabtree Contact series (Crabtree, 2009).

Garofoli, Wendy. *Hip-hop History*, Hip-hop USA series (Raintree, 2011).

Reynolds, Helen. A Fashionable History of ... series (Heinemann Library, 2004).

WEBSITES

www.ukbboy.info
    The UK's b-boy community website, containing news, moves, and info on competitions

www.britishhiphop.co.uk
    A website about British hiphop

www.commonsensemedia.org/music-review
    Go to the menu on the left of the page to find a list of hip-hop music for kids.

INDEX